To

Keira —

Love

auntie
Sylvia
+

MONOLOGUES

for

Youth

Volume 1

SYLVIA VALEVICIUS

B.A.,B.Ed.,M.A.,OCT

DEDICATION

To lovers of performance arts everywhere, and to the
wonderfully talented drama students who were in my classes, and
to those with future dreams of theatrical life.

CONTENTS

NOTICE

Occasionally, the grammar in these monologues strays from the expected rules in order to reflect the vernacular of youth. Thank you for noticing, Reader.

*All monologues are fictional creations. Any similarities to real people or situations are coincidental.

ACKNOWLEDGMENTS

My gratitude goes out, first, to my local Writers' Group members for their weekly sharing, their supportive comments, and brilliant ideas. Thank you to Craig for tech assistance and encouragement.

For their on-going phone support and conversation, I am grateful to cousin Maija, and friends, Lily, Monica, and my ever-laughing friend, as well as proof-reader, Sandie.

To my family, including Elaine and Oliver, for their enthusiasm, and to my thirteen grandchildren who are a constant source of imagination and inspiration in my heart - a huge thank you!

Finally, I want to thank the wonderful 'Indie' authors I found, read, and follow on Twitter. From these lovely writers, I include special mention to Catana Tully, and Jenny Lloyd. Their books, *Split at the Root*, and *Leap the Wild Water*, respectively, lit a fire under me..

THE CANDLE

(Girl, in white shirt, on stool, holding lighted candle. She could be 'sharing' in a youth psychotherapy group)

You know, everybody said "these are the best years of your life" when I turned eighteen last month. Mom and Pop took me out for dinner. At the restaurant, six other teenagers in white shirts and bow ties serenaded me, while holding a small piece of cake with one burning candle. I really felt embarrassed, especially since three of them – the singers – that is, went to my school. But I tried to look happy for Mom and Pop who were gushing and beaming the way adults do when they don't care what other people think.

You know, it's that one candle that stands out the most in my mind, though.

After Miss Hagan, my OAC English teacher kept hammering symbolism into our heads, I got to thinking – that candle, that one burning candle, means something.

I suddenly saw my entire eighteen years flash, or flicker, before me. My Gran used to tell me how my chubby little fist grabbed for the candle at my Christening – never mind that I was only eight weeks old! She told me that I was the brightest light in my parents' eyes that day.

At my First Communion, I remember walking down the aisle clutching my candle. I must have had a pained look on my face as I was carefully watching a drop of melting wax work its way down the ivory shaft. I looked up and saw Pop wink at me and I felt braver.

In case you're wondering, my connection to the single candle isn't all religious ceremonies, you know.

At my fifteenth birthday party, the neighborhood geek – turned street hunk -- came over. With his flaming red hair, Jamie, at sixteen, suddenly became every girl's dream. Here he was shaking hands with Mom and Pop and holding in his strong hands he had one gorgeous, pink candle. He turned to me and said:

"For you – no wonder your parents called you Dawn – your smile brightens up everybody's life – especially mine."

I nearly died! Can you imagine any sixteen year old guy being so romantic? And poetic? By the way, since then, Jamie has been so special in my life that no one will ever hold a candle to him!

Sorry, but for you non-English types that means Jamie's unbeatable. In fact, he's undefeatable and he's teaching me how to cope.

My Mom, Pop, Gran, and Jamie are behind me in this. Next week, I have my surgery. Jamie is donating his bone marrow to help cure my leukemia.

Yeah, maybe Mom and Pop are right. Maybe this is the best year of my life. Just maybe...

(She snuffs out candle)

(In the dark, she says):

Please light a candle for me, Jamie.

BLACKOUT

MONSTER BASH

(Seventeen year old boy testifies at an inquest)

Everybody wants to feel important, right? Even if they don't admit it. So, I thought hey! Here's my chance to get some recognition. Most of my friends are older. They let me hang out with them but I never felt like they really cared what I had to say. I was just there, you know, hanging out, a part of the group. Hell, I don't even have a driver's license so I couldn't impress any of them with my car like my buddy Steve. When you have a car, you've got buddies that need you to give them a lift somewhere. Let's face it, you're popular, you're cool. Well, that wasn't the case with me.

So when my parents had to fly to Vancouver for my dad's sister's wedding, they took my brother with them. He's just twelve. They wanted me to go too but I told them with exams coming up I really needed the time to study. They actually bought it!

My mom thought at sixteen I could stay home alone for a weekend and take care of myself – but she did leave me some dinners she made up, in the freezer. They left me phone numbers and all the usual stuff like lists of what to do and what not to do. My brother taped all the information on the frig door and gave me a snotty look, like you'd better do what mom says, or you're in for it. I was glad to get rid of him and the parents for a few days.

On that Friday at school, word got around that my parents would be out of town. I made sure that everyone knew that my place was the place to be for the hottest bash. In fact, I even made tickets and sold them for five bucks a head.

People started coming around 9:30. Our house isn't big but we have a two-storey and a pretty nice backyard, with a patio and pool. My dad insisted that's something he always wanted when he was a kid so he bought us this place six years ago. My mom kept it pretty nice but you kind of expect parents to look after their property. I never gave it much thought myself, except when I had to pay my brother off to cut the grass.

Anyway, the house started filling up pretty quickly and by about eleven, the forty people or so I expected quickly turned to around sixty. I didn't have to worry about too much noise or if the neighbors would call the cops because our house is sort of in the country – the next house would be about a city block away. So we blasted the speakers, the place filled up with smoke and the beer was plenty. A lot of people went outside because it was getting sweat mad hot inside from everybody dancing.

Actually, I felt great. Everybody kept telling me what a great guy I was to have them over. I have to admit that after about five beers, I didn't give a shit about little things like if people were using ashtrays or not. I just wanted everybody to have an amazing time. And they were!

But you know how it is when you drink beer – you have to piss so bad about every fifteen minutes. So I remember banging on the bathroom door to whoever was in there to hurry up and they let me in. Steve and some guys he knew from another school were in there and they were doing lines of snow. Christ! For a while I was scared but I thought what the hell, they're not hurting anyone – anyway it's not like anyone I knew was going to drink and drive. I expected most of them would just crash on the floor till the next day. I didn't want to ruin their fun or look like a sucky idiot.

The party lasted all night and I guess we musta had around a hundred and twenty people – half of them I didn't even know. By about four in the morning I was getting tired and I saw the place was getting trashed bad. I tried to encourage people to leave. A fight broke out over some chick - I didn't even know the guy - but I got in the way and had my nose bloodied. I looked around for Steve to help me clear the losers out but I couldn't find him anywhere.

I went outside to see if he was lying in the bushes somewhere. I didn't find him but I did see a couple making-out and in another spot some dude was lying in his puke.

I must of fallen asleep because I don't remember much else until the next day. Most of the people had left and I woke up the others and asked them to take off.

When I was finally alone, I felt a panic about the mess. I also felt Steve must of driven home even when he was stoned. I checked for his car and could see it was still parked down the road. I decided to sit for a while in the back, in the afternoon sunshine and have a smoke, you know, and think about what to do next.

Then I saw him. His blue shirt and jeans were sort of camouflaged by the dark water. The pool hadn't been cleaned yet for the summer. He was in the pool, just floating, face-down. I vomited what was left in my gut and began to shake so bad that my teeth felt like they were going to break.

I was still sitting there in a state of shock an hour later when our neighbor, Mr. Wallace, came by to check up on me. It seems my parents had asked him to. He called the authorities; they took Steve's body away.

Well, you know the rest. The autopsy showed that Steve had a heart attack from snorting too much coke. I guess as he had the 'coronary seizure' as they called it, he stumbled into the pool and everybody was too drunk or stoned to notice.

I never thought an eighteen year old could have a heart attack. I always thought that happened to old people.

Afterwards, for the longest time everybody at school would stare at me like I was some kind of monster. Nobody would really talk to me. I was the guy whose best friend died at my house, at my party.

I'm sorry for Steve and his family. I'm sorry that my parents no longer trust me.

Yeah, I guess I got the recognition I wanted...but not the kind I expected. (Pauses...hangs head.)

BLACKOUT

EXCUSES

(Teenage girl, out of breath, called into Principal's office)

Oh, my God, I'm sorry I'm late, sir. I know you said 8:30 sharp, but my mother just went into labor this morning and my dad was away on a business trip so I had to drive her and I've only got my beginners and we were pulled over for drunk driving.

Well, I mean my mother was the one drunk in the back seat. You see sir, she was in so much pain that I poured her a stiff shot before we left and then she was giving me these tipsy directions. Well, the officer escorted us to the hospital, rushed us in and then I had to fill out these forms for maternity and before I knew it somebody put <u>me</u> in the wheelchair – you see, sir, I was wearing this winter coat so you couldn't tell – and then they wheeled me up to the ward, put me into a room, and said the doctor will be with me shortly. They were so efficient I didn't have the heart to tell them they had the wrong patient.

Next thing I knew, my mother was my roommate 'cause she got wheeled in right after me. Well, right then and there, sir, I decided to clear things up, kissed my mom goodbye and was about to head for school when I realized in all the excitement that I had forgotten my books at home.

When I went in the back door that leads to the kitchen, I could smell coffee, and right then and there, sir, I knew there was trouble! You see, sir, I hate coffee and my mom couldn't stomach it when she was pregnant. My cat does tricks, but she's not *that* clever. I figured right then and there, sir, that there was an intruder hanging about. So I booted it out of there so fast – didn't wait around to find out who he was and headed over to my neighbor Alice Crum's place.

The both of us called the police and when they got there twenty minutes later, they wanted me to make a statement. So I stated: 'What the hell took you so long?'' Sorry, sir, but what would *you* do?

Anyway, they went to my place and found my *dad* in his bathrobe coming out of the shower. They started to put handcuffs on him until I screamed "Daddy!" Then they told me I was a troublemaker. I mean, you can't win, can you?

Well, right then and there, we cleared things up and I was about to leave for school when the phone rang and it was the hospital telling us that my brother's leg looks good and that they won't have to operate after all. Of course, I thought my mom had a baby boy with an extra leg. I told daddy we had a boy and we both rushed back to the hospital to congratulate my mom and well, we were disappointed because there was no baby, just false labor and we had to bring mom back home.

Oh, the boy with the leg, well, I'm embarrassed, sir, but I put our phone number on the wrong forms.

Well, my dad just dropped me off at school now and when I went to my locker it was stuck, so I kicked it just a bit and it flew open and the teeniest little mouse raced out with a piece of my old, cheese sandwich trailing him. It sort of scared Miss Noble who was passing by and I had to help her off the floor 'cause she passed out. She didn't even realize that she fell on the mouse and killed the little guy herself. Well, right there and then, sir, I told her I was in a bit of a hurry 'cause I had to meet you, so you can see, sir, I'm not trying to make excuses for being late. I realize that right here and now, sir that I have to clear things up. Sir?

BLACKOUT

PERFECT DECISIONS

(Teenage girl makes some changes in her life)

Look at me. Don't I look perfect? I mean, I'm dressed well. A wool sweater, pure virgin woolen skirt – this touch of pearls – so fifties glam, isn't it? Well, I may not look like your average teenager. I'm not sure that I am.

Since I am their only child, my parents set high standards for me - so I get good grades. I'm accomplished in my piano. I'm even vice-president of the student council at my school this semester. My parents always advised me to make the right decisions, to choose well for my future. I know that I am an adult- in- training.

I have to say my parents were always there for me. Well, they even have the right guy picked out for me when the time is right, they say. Only they won't say who he is. When I had problems, mom and dad were always in my corner. They were proud of me, and I of them too. Until last year.

Last summer I fell from grace. Why? I let myself fall in love with a boy who worked as a counselor with me at the *Kids Camp for the Physically Challenged*. Most of the kids at the camp were of Aboriginal descent.

You're probably wondering what's wrong with falling in love. I guess nothing - for most people. But for me it was an emotional explosion that I never before allowed myself to feel. I always used to believe that that type of love is irrational and that it wasn't for me to feel so out of control.

But it was the most wonderful experience of my life to care about someone else instead of focusing on myself. To listen to him, his concerns, and to talk with him for long star-lit hours into the night while sitting by a glowing campfire, at the forest's edge.

My parents were shocked and disappointed when I found myself pregnant. Well, I was shocked too. I never thought this could happen, but when two people melt into one, well, you know the rest. I just found it hard to believe it, myself. I was not quite ready for this – not yet grown-up.

After they got over their initial alarm, my parents were only too willing to help me. Even though he might have become the boy of my teenage dreams, Albert Sage, also an Aboriginal young man, was not their choice for me. He was less than perfect in their eyes for their little girl. I never understood why. He was beautiful, smart, and kind.

Mom and dad said not to worry. They would help me with my decision. So they decided I would have an abortion. Their *baby* would not suffer the disgrace of premature childbirth.

Since that time I still look the same on the outside – just habit I guess – but inside I'm different.

For once, I made my own decision. I decided to continue with my pregnancy. My parents almost disowned me because I brought shame into their lives. I was no longer their perfect little girl.

(Smiles)

But there is a perfect little girl that I handed over to her young father last month. He and his hard-working family welcomed and treasured little Alberta Joy into their lives.

(Pause) I visit her from time to time.

I guess that decision was the most perfect one I ever made. Did I mention I'm happy? I gave my child a choice and a chance to really live, and...well...I can live with that decision.

BLACKOUT

CYBERFACE

(Teen girl's experiences with Internet)

I was eleven years old when I **lied** my way onto Facebook. I was living with my dad at the time and he was so busy with his own internet dating websites that he paid little attention to what **I** was doing on-line.

Before Facebook, I went on websites where I could buy my own condo, decorate it with the coolest furniture, like leather couches and other gorgeous stuff. Then I chose an Avatar that looks like me. I gotta tell ya, my Avatar was super sexy – of course - she didn't even look eleven, but more like seventeen. Naturally, I picked the cutest outfits to wear, miniskirts and cropped tops, and hot pink sneakers, and then

I waited for others to show up.

After a while I got bored with inviting other Avatars to visit me in my condo – they never felt like real people even though real people were behind them, creating them. I was itching to get on Facebook.

Wow! What a world opened up to me!

Suddenly I was collecting 'friends' I didn't even know because they were friends of friends. Crazy, eh? My friends from my old neighborhood were on, too. Kevin from our last townhouse complex posted a photo of himself without a shirt on – I felt a little strange seeing that, I must admit. It wasn't like he was wearing pajamas, either.

Soon I was feeling comfortable enough to express my feelings. I posted various pouty poses of myself asking people to 'like' me. I told everyone I was feeling depressed when sometimes I wasn't, just to see what they would say. I loved the attention. Who wouldn't?

Lots of my classmates joined too. We made up phoney birth dates and nobody caught us. At least, no Facebook police.

But one day things turned strange. People started to say mean things to me. Some girls said they were not going to be friends with me anymore. They started to tell me I looked dumb and needy. What's needy? I thought.

Well ... that was the problem. Just about every thought that went through my head I posted on Facebook. I wanted to share my life with everybody out there. I even said that I was thinking of *killing* myself. I hoped for sympathy and more friends. Then --a big surprise! People were posting stuff like: **Do it! Do it**! I felt hated. They hated me!

Someone even called me an idiot. I can't believe they were bullying me. You're not supposed to do that! And friends of Kevin's older brother – guys in their twenties said they had *something to show* me, in private. It was sickening

I didn't want to tell my dad or he would kill me, for sure!

Lucky for me, my Aunt Betsy, who lives in another Province – Nova Scotia – spotted me one day as I tried to fight back with the bullies and gently advised me to close my account.

Then she got my email and wrote me a kind letter. She said, Isabella, it's not safe for young girls to open themselves up to strangers, and to post those type of photos – which she called *revealing*.

I like my Aunt Betsy so I listened to her, and removed myself for almost two years from Facebook. I got to understand what the word *discreet* means, and learned that over-sharing can be dangerous.

Now that I am fifteen, I've been back on Facebook for a while, and Instagram too, with pictures of my favorite things. Mostly, that's my adorable, miniature wiener dog, *Thunder**. He's such a beauty and can be so silly. He has lots of Facebook 'likes' these days when he's wearing his Santa's Elf Cap. It's fun dressing *him* up for attention, instead of myself.

Growing up is never easy they used to say – now I *know* what *they* mean .Especially in our digital, cyber world. Yeah, but it's sick!   (Big smile – two thumbs up!)

BLACKOUT

Description of Thunder's cap can change depending on season – Halloween, etc.

LOCKDOWN

(Teenage boy reflects on a crisis)

My cousin Barry clapped his hand over my mouth and pulled me to the floor. It felt like he ripped my shoulder, he was so fierce and fast, like the running back he is.

It didn't take me long to realize we were in danger of losing our lives. Just the screaming outside in the hallway. And the shots. I'd never heard shots before in my life, just the ones from TV, and man, is it ever different!

Other kids were hiding under desks, silent, scared shitless. Barry and me were up near the blackboard, at the front of the room, and out of sight – at least from the window of the classroom door.

Me and Barry had been giving a seminar together when this happened. It was our Civics class that we had together and we were presenting on Good Citizenship and all that boring stuff.

I'm a smaller guy than Barry, smaller frame, but we're the same age. Our dads are brothers. Barry got the size of *my* dad, and I just hadn't caught up yet. I was lucky he was there for me that day.

Every cliché you could think of was happening in real life, happening so fast. My pulse suddenly was in my throat throbbing like I'd swallowed my heart. I'd never experienced such fear.

And where was Miss Walters? She was not in the class with us. Where did she disappear to?

Then the PA blared – I mean blared! violent sounds from the 70's heavy metal rock band - Led Zeppelin – their song, 'Whole Lotta Love' was perverted. Some weirdoes had taken over the front office address- system and blasted the guttural sex part of that song – you know, that 'ah-ah-ah-ah-ah' – it was sickening. All over the school, gunshots, and that sound. I can never, ever, listen to Robert Plant again, after that. Perverted!

Barry told me later that I fainted soon after. I felt like such a girl hearing that. Barry reminded me that my heart pace-maker that I got at eight months old must have triggered my collapse, given the ordeal.

This was a moment in my teenage life that I'm afraid I will never forget.

We later learned that three people were gunned down in the hallway outside our door before the SWAT team intercepted. One of those was our sweet Miss Walters who rushed to lock our classroom door, but ran over to help a girl to safety who was stumbling with crutches – that was Christine, after her ski accident, a friend of ours.

They were both killed along with Fred, our school's caretaker and everyone's buddy.

Now when I hear the word *lockdown*, I have flashbacks. And we have 'lockdown' drills all the time! Going to school is not the crazy fun times we used to have anymore. It's a whole different kind of crazy now.

It was hard returning to school after two weeks shutdown.

Barry and me, we were talking...we think when we grow up and have kids, we're gonna 'home-school' them. Or maybe we'll open our own small private school one day and call it CFW Academy, after those we loved, who died that day.

BLACKOUT

CUTS AND BRUISES

(Girl speaks to a youth-therapy group)

Adam squeezed me hard. He said he intended to love me forever.

Forever? I laughed in his face. We're only sixteen. You might be sick of me by next semester.

I don't like it when other guys look at you, he said. Maybe you shouldn't wear those cut-offs. Everyone's looking at your ass. [Could substitute the word 'butt']

We were sitting in his mom's basement and he was fumbling with the pearly buttons on my jean-shirt. I tried to sweetly push him away but his forearms were so strong. You can't mess with Adam – he's on the school wrestling team,

and he wins each time.

We had only been seeing each other for a few weeks and he always seemed such a gentleman. Fortunately, he left my buttons, too slippery for his thick fingers, I guess, and went to stroke my hair. Suddenly he yanked my ponytail – he yanked it hard! And it hurt. When I said owww, he said that's what happens to bad girls who show too much around.

Then he pulled a small jackknife – like a Swiss Army type – from his back pocket, flicked it open and said he wanted to show me how he's mine forever. He wanted to make a nick in my arm. Before I could protest, he scratched the slant of an 'A' for Adam inside my wrist.

Stop it! Stop it! I screamed at him. I knew no one would hear me though, because we were alone in the house, downstairs.

There was blood. He licked it off. He joked that he was a vampire. I didn't find it funny.

By now, I was crying. He told me to cut it out. I cried more, getting afraid. Then he slapped me hard across the face – to sober me up he said.

Thank God his parents came home when they did, in through the garage door with their groceries. I didn't say anything. I was too scared and ashamed. I had my jacket on to cover myself, said a quick hello to his dad, and before I took off, Adam's mom who was further away up in the kitchen said that my face looked red and was I coming down with something. Little did they know.

I told Adam I was mad at him, and needed some space. At school he stared at me in the caf when I sat with my girlfriends. He just kept staring in a creepy way two tables over. Everybody just thought we'd had a fight and didn't press me for more info.

So last Thursday night, I was home alone because my parents had to go with my younger sister, Sally, to parent/teacher night.

The doorbell began ringing like it was some emergency, without pausing, over and over. I peeked through a corner of the living room drapes and could see it was Adam out there. My stomach just turned to knots, my mouth dry. He looked weird. I thought he might be drunk, and I was scared.

He started shouting, "Let me in, Eve. I know you're there. Let me in. We belong together." He knew my parents were out, plus no car in the driveway. He said, "I'll find a way in, Eve." His voice was ugly and coarse.

I was in full panic mode, grabbed the kitchen phone, and locked myself in the bathroom, where I called 911.

Sirens blared outside in about four minutes. Through a megaphone some officer in the front yard was speaking to me, telling me that I am safe and can let them in now. Adam was restrained in a police car.

I later learned from my parents that Adam had a lot of strange instruments and magazines hidden under his bed at home. My parents got all the updates from the authorities, and told me there are things about Adam I shouldn't know.

All I could figure out was that Adam was pitiful. He imagined us as Adam and Eve. How crazy is that? That's why I am in therapy now, learning to deal with an over-controlling boyfriend, and possibly one with a mental illness that we kids call *schizoid*.

Adam and Eve? **OMG** – I feel like I should change my name now. No longer be Eve, anymore, but return to being called, Evelyn, as I was named at birth. (Pause)

Or maybe... I'll just go by my middle name - Elizabeth. What do you think? Can't mess with a Queen! Right guys? (Nervous laughter all round)

BLACKOUT

THE HIJAB

(Girl speaks to school Guidance Counselor)

You know, Mrs. Conway, we, my family, came from Pakistan six years ago.

My English is pretty good because we studied hard.

I couldn't wait to move here to Canada – live free like the other girls.

But my family, especially my father, is very religious and my older brother Khamal is just like him. Well, Khamal is mean and bossy. And my mother is so quiet. She never sticks up for herself to my dad. She never sticks up for me, either. She just looks at me with her blank eyes and her sad face, and watches me carefully every morning that I put my hijab on correctly.

Pretty soon I started to go into the girls' washroom, here at school, and took off my hijab. The other girls in my class encouraged me to when I was complaining about wearing it. They said let's see your hair. They said my hair is so thick and long and shiny. They were telling me it's beautiful and that the color matches my dark chestnut eyes. Gosh, I loved hearing that, the way they compared my hair to my eyes, and compared my eyes to part of Canadian nature. We don't have chestnuts in Pakistan. (A small laugh)

Of course, I was scared to go back into the classroom after that – I mean – my head uncovered. I put back my hijab – what if a teacher would tell my parents?

My father would kill me for not wearing the hijab. I don't mean he would kill me like the kids say here all the time – my parents will kill me if I don't finish my homework – that sort of stuff. I mean my father and his spy, Khamal, would *really* kill me if they knew. They would strangle me with my own scarf. They are angry people, my father and brother. They would make me dead, Mrs. Conway.

I know you find this hard to understand, or even believe, Mrs. Conway, but it's true.

So, I'll tell you what I did. Well, you know some of it.

I don't go home anymore. I moved into Michelle's house with her mom who's really cool. We left a voice message for Khamal that I am staying with friends for a while and please not to worry.

Michelle and her mom took me shopping for jeans, and they even took me to that big make-up store in the mall. They took me to a hairdresser, too, who loved my hair. I didn't let on that I used to wear a hijab. I wanted to act cool.

Mrs. Conway, I just want to be like a normal Canadian girl.

Michelle helped me open a Facebook account and we took lots of pictures of ourselves. I wasn't worried at all about that because my parents don't go on to a computer, and they don't know anything about Facebook. They spend a lot of time praying.

So, my parents know that I am staying with a friend for a few weeks, yes, but I can't stay at Michelle's forever.

Can you help me get into a foster home, Mrs. Conway? One where my parents won't be able to find me? I can't go back home. I won't dress like that ever again. I want to be a free human being. If I go home, like I said, my father will kill me.

Would you help me please? Help me to stay *alive*, Mrs. Conway?

BLACKOUT

SHRINK ME

(Boy, 15, at visit with psychiatrist)

I'm not talking. (Pause) I'm not talking. (Pause) I'm not talking to you, Doc. I don't *have* to talk to you. Just because my parents sent me here, doesn't mean I have to talk to you. (Pause)

You can stare all you want, Doc. I'm just going to chew a piece of *Juicy Fruit*. (He unwraps a stick of gum taken from his pocket, and begins chewing) Is that alright, Ladies? Okay, just a joke. Don't you 'get' kid slang, Doc? Aren't you supposed to be a 'child psychiatrist'? Well, chew on this, Doc, I'm no child, but my parents, mad creatures that they are, think I'm on drugs.

Wonder why they think that, eh, Doc? Any ideas? Why do you keep staring at me? And what are you writing, anyway? Love letter to your wife? Maybe just the grocery list, 'cause I don't really think you're listening to me, just faking interest for all the mint you must be pulling in trying to make me talk.

Look, my Fam is all effed up – mad effed! You should be talking to them, Doc. Not me.

What do you want me to tell you, anyway? – even if I wanted to talk – which I don't...

You think I'm crazy, Doc? You gonna slap a label on me and keep the folks happy?

Maybe I'll tell you what bugs me, Doc. People who try to get into my head space. Tell me this. Tell me that. Why are you late? Why are your eyes red?

Are your eyes red, Doc? Mine are red from studying too hard, Doc. That's what I tell my mom. She's too stoned, herself, to notice much.

Talk about drugs – my old lady is on Valium or some shit like that twenty-four seven. And she wants *me* to see a shrink? God! what a laugh. She's so effin' messed up.

And my dad – he's a grind. Comes home loaded every night – his eyes more glazed than a Thanksgiving Ham. All dressed nice in his business suit, except for little smudges of pink on his neck behind his ears – keeps his necktie clean -

. His boozy smell picks up something stronger when he removes his suit jacket. I think the polite phrase would be 'women of the night' smell. Course you wouldn't know what that is like, Doc, probably happily married. One of the lucky ones, right, Doc?

Sometimes we're lucky when my dad doesn't swing at us with a baseball bat. The A-hole is always so pissed. Maybe one of these days, my effin dad will remember what the bloody thing is really used for. When did you last play ball with me, ' *dad* '?

Well, my mother had to go and open her big mouth, Doc. My older brother Anthony, who sells Real Estate – and still lives at home - overheard a huge fight between my parents last month. And he told me - Marcus, you won't believe this shit, man, but I care about you. You're my bro, dude. Why all this love fest, all of a sudden, I wondered.

It happens the parents came home early one afternoon. I was at school and Anthony's girlfriend, Carla, dropped him off, and then took his car to get her nails done, or some shit like that. Anthony stayed in the basement office filling out some paperwork. She was gonna pick him up later.

So Brian and Mary come in early from some phony bank lunch of his, and have it out, after too many Martinis. Mom tells him that when we lived in New York - I wasn't born yet - she was five months preggers with me – her coworker turned lover, died in the World Trade Centre disaster of 9-11. She was at the hairdressers that morning. She had so much pain and guilt. She was going to tell *'Dad'* and leave him. But since the boyfriend died, actually his name was Sheldon, Ma had a good way of hiding everything. I was born as *Dad's* kid, when we moved back to Canada. But she couldn't stand it anymore, so she blabbed it all out that afternoon.

So, Brian's no more my dad than you are, Doc. Who the hell am I, Doc? Why did she have to tell him that? My dad is not my dad. My grandparents are not my grandparents. What the eff am I, doc? A World Trade Centre kid? Who am I?

Why did she have to lay it out there, true confession, style, like some friggin' 'reality show' and mess my life with her effin 'truth'?

So go head, Doc. Dissect my brain like the little frogs we ripped apart in science class. Do your magic, because I don't know who I am, anymore. Shrink me!! Doc.

BLACKOUT

COPYCAT

(Girl makes a video YouTube message)

We were famous. Three of us always together. Ours is just a small-town community with one elementary school, and one secondary. People know each other quite well.

Earlier this year, Bonnie, Todd, and me, Alicia, started grade eight together, all brand new teenagers, our birthdays being a couple of months apart. Thirteen sounded pretty good to us. And of course, we were in the same class. This year we were finally at the 'top of the heap' as my dad puts it. We talked a lot about grad coming up, and prom clothes. We were stoked for this fun year!

People called us *The Three Musketeers*, after some

swashbucklers in a classic novel. Actually, we thought of ourselves more like the three *Mouseketeers*, from the *Disney* shows of the 1960's that we found on TV reruns. We loved *Disney* stuff and promised each other never to outgrow it. Todd said he'd love *Disney* forever because he intended to grow into a Prince, not telling us which one. I thought maybe the one that wakes 'Sleeping Beauty?' Todd told us once that his middle name is Phillip - after his uncle.

So, seeing the fun we were having, the grades sevens, sixes, fives, all wanted to copy us, how we talked, making up our own text slang, how we dressed, wearing our long johns to school, our team toques, and how we stickered up our backpacks. Never mind how cool we made our lockers, posting our selfies of the three of us making crazy faces that everyone stopped to stare at when they passed in the hallway.

And we were pranksters! No one was safe with us around. And Todd was filled with ideas for our field trip to Ottawa – which was such a fun time and we laughed staying up as late as possible until Miss Franks and Mr. Lovett, our chaperones, told us to chill out. We loved doing celebrity parodies, their habits, and songs. Our specialty was *Justin Bieber*. Even though he's from a small town in Ontario, too, we were definitely NOT fans, so we would imitate him in silly ways, parody his boy-dance style.

We were fans of *Taylor Swift*, and the older girl, *Avril*

Lavigne, another small-town kid who made it big. We had dreams for ourselves, too. Me and Bonnie were in dance, went to provincial competitions and Todd, did vocals and guitar with some of his buddies.

We used to say that the best always comes from little towns – except for that *Biebster* that we picked on 'cause he was always getting himself into stupid trouble - like with the law – so we labeled him a loser, even with all his money. We'd say he'd come to no good one day.

A couple of months ago, things changed for us. Bonnie and Todd developed huge crushes on each other and were taking selfies of just the two of them. They even called it 'dating' – even though they never went anywhere alone like grown-ups do. I wasn't even jealous; I didn't mind. I was really so busy with assignments, and dance practice. I knew my time as a *Mousketeer* was coming to an end. Bonnie and Todd would text each other like crazy and I'd see some of their stuff on Facebook. I still loved the both of them to bits.

Two weeks ago, Todd was devastated. Nothing anything kids our age should know or hear. He told Bonnie that his Uncle Alistair, (who's Uncle Phillip's younger brother) died.

Wait! It gets worse. I won't say 'it 'get's better' like they say these days because, this uncle that Todd went snowboarding and fly-fishing with, spent so much time with, *killed* himself.

That's right. Suicide. Who can even *say* that word without being creeped out? Todd told me and Bonnie that his uncle hanged himself – sort of like the comedian who played *Mrs. Doubtfire - Robin Williams*, with his own pants' belt.

Todd was shocked, depressed, sad, and just couldn't understand why his uncle did this.

I think Todd was trying to figure this out. I think Todd tried to *imitate* what that was like – how far one can go to choke himself. (BIG PAUSE)

Todd died a week after his uncle. Todd died by his own hand. He copied his uncle.

His mother went on Facebook and told people Todd had an accident, and we will all miss him.

Bonnie and me were hysterical. There's no other way of putting it – when we heard about Todd. What was he thinking? We would never really know.

That was the end of our three *Mouseketeers*, forever. Poor Bonnie couldn't see straight she was in so much grief and pain. Todd was her *first* boyfriend. He was just thirteen, a good kid.

Of course, it seemed like the entire town turned up at the funeral to bury one of its own kids. Todd was in an open casket, looking so alive, just sleeping, as they say.

I got up the courage, somehow, to speak about Todd about how sweet and funny he was and how much he meant to us all, and how he played his tricks on the teachers, and how they really loved it, but pretended to be annoyed.

My grandma who lives in Toronto texted me that I was brave and kind, to do this. Thanks, Gran.

I think it's time to stop copying others, and just be yourself. Todd is probably with the angels and pulling his famous jokes on them. Still famous. Without us. We miss you, Toddie.

And you guys out there – I just want to add – don't be copycats. (Pause) Please.

BLACKOUT

WORD PUZZLE

(Boy Tells Classmates Family Anecdote)

"Mom!" I said bringing in the mail. "Ryan's SICK!"

'What wrong with Ryan? She comes rushing out from the laundry room with a worried look on her face, flipping one sock into another.

My mother is cool, but she still speaks '80's –

"No worries, Mom" I say. I try to explain that 'sick' is '80's 'sharp'.

"Ryan's hockey photos came in and he looks great, Mom. That's so sick!"

(Big Sigh)

Teaching your parents how to update their language skills is tricky, lemme tell ya!

I mean when my sister Violet got the 'A plus', for the debating team this morning, I told Mom Violet was stoked, on fire, and Mom was like "What happened to my baby?" She was practically hysterical.

I tried to reassure, Mom.

"Hey, Dude," I say, "no worries," but before I can finish, she interrupts me, and chirps –"Don't you mean, Dudette?"

"Nah, Mom," I tell her. "Dude is for you or dad. You Dudes own this place, so you're both the Dudes. And Violet's fine; she's just excited for her group's good mark. In fact, she's killin' it right now in the yard; her and Pansy," I say, looking out the kitchen window.

"WHAT? What are they killing" Mom shouts coming up the stairs. "Not the Joneses' pink hamster? Not neighborly at all. Oh, that Pansy of ours!"

"It's KK, Mom," they are just having fun doing handstands."

BTW, Pansy's our cat.

This explaining was getting to be hard work. I was thinking I should have stayed in my room with my headphones on...

Just then, Violet comes in and says, "Well, can I get an AMEN?" Mom turns to me and says, "Did she *bury* something in the yard, Connor?"

Violet, looking all confused says once again: "Can I get an AMEN? Mom? Connor?"She looks to both of us – "Duh? My A plus! I'm mad chill."

"That means she's happy, Mom," I tell her.

"I caught that," says Mom, giving me a smug look. Parents learn fast!

So Mom and me together say, "AMEN!" We congratulate Violet for her high, debating mark. High fives all around.

Then Mom says, "Violet, why are you dressed like that, honey?" Aren't those your PJ bottoms?"

"Mom, it's 'Flannel Friday.'" Violet tells her.

"And that means ...Connor?" Mom laughs, like she's enjoying these lessons, now.

Together me and mom say: "Wear - flannel – on - Fridays!"

But now, here comes the strange part:

Then Mom says, "Well, is that a *thing?*" She checks her finger nails, like cool mom-style

"Hey, awesome, Mom!"   I 'm impressed with her phrasing.

Nice timing. Ryan comes in through the garage door, hears this, grabs his photos from my hands and says: "I taught her *hash tag* 'everything she knows'. Am I right, Ladies?"

Well, that's an Instagram of our epic Fam. (Pause)

And, do you need me to explain this, guys? (Big smile – shrug – palms up)

BLACKOUT

CRUSHED

(Boy explains an incident at school to a therapy group)

I was stoked and a bit nervous when my parents decided I was going to attend a private high school. Okay, I've had some focus, concentration problems in grade school, so my folks thought a smaller environment, one-on-one attention, would be good for me.

The school was amazing. Basically, it was in the woods. A few low buildings for classes, and some for dorms, and we had a huge cottage type of A- frame structure for dining hall and recreation. And, of course, for all winter sports, we had skiing, mountain climbing, and in warm weather, Lake Renaissance that edged up to the docks by our school, was perfect for canoeing and kayaking.

The changing seasons, like the changing moods of our hearts, brought a sense of beauty and peace to the area. We had fresh breezes off the lake in spring, in autumn the grounds piled up with rusty golden leaves – we'd jump in and toss them around like little kids. In winter, the birches crystallized their branches into laser-style icicles. We'd snap them off and play fight with them, too. But mostly it was just a gorgeous and romantic place to study, or not... when your mind wandered.

I know, I know, it sounds poetic, but I'm known as that sort of guy! They call me deep and quiet, even though I enjoy a good time. My guidance adviser, Mr. Brookfield, calls me 'introspective.'

Anyway, grades nine and ten went okay. I had a roommate from Japan, one year: Shintero, nice guy, and he'd always say *'So, desnay?'* meaning, 'Is that right?' which he'd say with his eyes so wide; that became my phrase, too, all that year. The next year, in grade ten, I had a guy from Argentina, and he kept saying, *'Cayate!'* which means 'shut up' and he'd like to say that when guys were making a racket on our floor. That's Alfonso, and he's not all that quiet himself. But he was a good guy who taught me some great tango steps. He was known at our school as the 'ladies man'.

Our teachers at *Woodside Heights College* were cool, and yeah, nice to kids. It's like people really cared. Most of them lived in homes on the school grounds. Some teachers were even married couples like Mr. and Mrs. Brookfield.

You're probably wondering why I'm not talking about girls, right? Well, I'm not gay, but if I was, I'd tell you about a special guy, if I had one.

Actually, there were some cute girls at my school, yeah. Many were day students, bused in from the regional villages. Lots of the girls became my friends, and some of them even got crushes on me. I had a crush on one or two for a while, myself. Some girls posted on their Facebook and Instagram that they loved Charlie's ears. True, I must admit, I do have big ears.

Besides those ears, I'm told that I'm not bad-looking being tall and blond, and sure I stay in shape cause I work out – that's just a discipline I developed from being an Air Cadet leader for the last few years. I guess it gives me some straight posture, shit like that.

So, Mr. Brookfield was not only my adviser but also my homeroom and science teacher in grade eleven. And Mrs. B., his wife, taught me English and math. She was smart that way. She gave me extra attention and after-class help with math, and my essays. I really appreciated that.

Actually, I really liked Mrs. B. (*slows down*)

Pretty soon, I found I liked her too much. I liked her so much I felt sick. I started smashing things around in my bedroom in the dorm, and the other guys were like, WTF?

Part of me knew this feeling I had for Mrs. B. was crazy, wrong, (sigh) but another part of me was thrilled with longing. It was a feeling I couldn't handle because I knew it could never be returned to me. Like we learned in Shakespeare, the term 'unrequited love' was happening to me, and I had no control over it. She couldn't possibly love me back. In fact, she was six months pregnant with their first baby. Pregnant! That's how crazy it was in my mind. I didn't care that she was pregnant. I just knew that I loved her, her sweet voice, and her gentle manner. She was my world.

After I pretty much destroyed my bedroom, the freaked-out floor supervisors had the principal call my parents, and tell them to take me home before they call the police.

So I'm in therapy now. Crazy, alright. For falling in love. With an inappropriate person. A married, pregnant teacher who is maybe only ten years older than me. It *could* work, but I'm not supposed to think that way. It sucks! Bad!! (Closes eyes)

BLACKOUT

ABOUT THE AUTHOR

Sylvia Valevicius is a mother, grandmother, reader, and writer. She is a sometime actor, known as Joey T. Oliver. Former English Literature and Dramatic Arts secondary school teacher, Sylvia directed school dramas and musical theatre during her career with three school boards in Ontario.

Sylvia enjoys social media. You can find her on Twitter as: @Jtosnest

Sylvia lives in Oakville, Ontario.

37730382R10040

Made in the USA
Charleston, SC
15 January 2015